I0018775

Vibe Coding, The Coming Wave

"It is the obvious which is so difficult to see most of the time. People say 'It's as plain as the nose on your face.' But how much of the nose on your face can you see, unless someone holds a mirror up to you?"
— Isaac Asimov, I, Robot

Chapter 1: The Birth of the Vibe – A New Era or Just the Next Hype?

Okay, let's be honest: How many times have we heard that *now* everything is changing? Every time, there's a new buzzword bingo, new consultants, new frameworks promising the moon – almost as if someone handed us Rita Skeeter's Quick-Quotes Quill, writing everything automatically while... well, creatively interpreting the truth. Agile, DevOps, Microservices, the Cloud... You get a bit jaded over time. You know the design patterns in your sleep, you're familiar with the pitfalls of legacy systems, and you've survived more refactorings than you can count sprint plannings.

And now? Now comes "Vibe Coding." At first, it sounds like something you'd overhear at a tech festival between two keynotes while trying to grab the free coffee. But something feels different this time, doesn't it? This underlying feeling that it's not just about *how* we write code, but *whether* we need to write it at all. In online forums and at conferences, you can sense this strange mix of gold-rush fever and quiet panic. Is this just the next hype, or the beginning of a real revolution?

What the Heck is "Vibe Coding"?

Let's picture this: You're no longer sitting there typing line by line, battling stubborn semicolons, obscure compiler errors, and the documentation of a library last updated in 2018. Instead, perhaps you lean back comfortably (maybe with that aforementioned coffee) and *talk* to your development environment. You describe what you need – not in precise pseudo-code or a formal specification, but in plain language. "Hey AI, build me an API that pulls user data from the old Oracle DB, enriches it with info from the new NoSQL thingy, and spits it out as JSON. Oh, and make it secure, okay?"

And the thing... does it. At least in theory, or increasingly often in practice. That's the core idea of "Vibe Coding": An Artificial Intelligence, usually a Large Language Model (LLM) trained on code (like models from OpenAI, Anthropic, Google, or open-source alternatives), takes your natural language instructions – your "vibes" – and translates them into executable code. Your role changes dramatically: You're no longer the bricklayer painstakingly placing one brick upon another, but rather the planner, the architect, the technical lead, designing the blueprint, guiding the AI, critically reviewing the result, and saying, "Nope, that wall needs to be a bit further left, and the foundation looks shaky." You become the orchestrator, the tamer of artificial intelligence.

The term was likely coined by Andrej Karpathy, one of the well-known figures in the AI scene, in early 2025. His description hits the nail on the head: It's about "fully embracing the vibes, embracing the exponential, and forgetting that the code even exists." Sounds tempting and a bit terrifying at the same time, right? Forgetting the code exists? Us? The people who can spend nights hunting down an obscure memory leak or optimizing the intricacies of an algorithm?

Some see Vibe Coding as the logical next step from Low-Code/No-Code platforms, just using natural language instead of graphical building blocks. Others, like the venerable Merriam-Webster dictionary, define it with a hint of irony as "carefree coding with AI assistance where the programmer doesn't have to understand how it works." Ouch. But even this perhaps somewhat critical definition holds a kernel of truth: It's another powerful layer of abstraction. After assembler, high-level languages, and frameworks, now come... the vibes. The stated goal of many of these new approaches: A development environment where AI agents become our daily programming buddies.

The gist: We talk to the machine, it spits out code. Simple in concept, but potentially revolutionary in impact. The line between developer and tool, between instruction and collaboration, blurs here in an unprecedented way.

From Punch Cards to Prompt Poets: The Evolution of Programming

This idea of simplifying and abstracting programming isn't new. It's practically the DNA of computer science history. Let's briefly recall the wild ride that brought us here:

- **The Primordial Era (ca. 1940s-1960s):** Punching cards, plugging wires, flipping switches, entering direct machine commands. Programming was a highly specialized, almost elitist craft for a handful of mathematicians and engineers in white lab coats. Finding errors was a disaster, the hardware was enormous and sinfully expensive. Any abstraction, however small, was a blessing.

- **Assembler & Early High-Level Languages (1950s-1970s):** Names like FORTRAN, COBOL, LISP, and BASIC emerged. A huge leap! Suddenly, one could think in more human-like commands (at least to some extent). Assembler provided a thin, symbolic layer over cryptic machine code.

This made software development accessible to a broader audience, but it remained complex and error-prone. The infamous spaghetti code, often caused by excessive use of GOTO statements, was commonplace.

- **Structured Programming (1970s):** Visionaries like Edsger Dijkstra recognized the dangers of unstructured code ("GOTO considered harmful!"). Fundamental control structures like sequence, selection (if/else), and iteration (loops), along with the concept of subroutines/functions, were established. Languages like Pascal and C implemented these ideas consistently. The goal: More readable, maintainable, and testable code. A milestone for software quality.

- **Object-Oriented Programming (OOP) (1980s-1990s):** With languages like Smalltalk, C++, and later the giants Java and C#, the world was broken down into objects encapsulating data (attributes) and behavior (methods). Concepts like classes, inheritance, and polymorphism promised to manage complexity

6

better, increase reusability, and facilitate the construction of large, modular systems. OOP still dominates many areas of software development today, although its concepts have sometimes been dogmatically overused.

- **The Web and Scripting Languages (1990s-2000s):** The internet exploded, and suddenly the world needed dynamic websites and applications. HTML defined the structure, but languages like JavaScript, PHP, Perl, Python, and Ruby brought life to the party. Scripting languages often made development faster and more flexible, but also led to new chaos ("Callback Hell" in JavaScript, anyone?). Frameworks like Ruby on Rails, Django, Spring, and later in the frontend Angular, React, and Vue attempted to bring structure and productivity back to web development.
- **Agile & DevOps (2000s-Present):** The realization dawned that technology alone isn't everything. Process and culture are at least as important. Agile methodologies with shorter iterations, closer collaboration, and more

flexibility replaced rigid waterfall models. DevOps brought development and operations together, focusing on automating build, test, and deployment processes (CI/CD) and fostering a culture of rapid feedback and continuous improvement.

- **AI Assistance (ca. 2015-Present):** The tools got smarter. Intelligent code completion in IDEs, increasingly sophisticated linters and static analysis tools, refactoring helpers. And then came the first true AI pair programmers like GitHub Copilot (powered initially by OpenAI Codex). AI became the assistant, taking over routine tasks, suggesting code, and sometimes even detecting errors.

And now, after all these stages, we stand before **Vibe Coding**. It's the (provisional?) peak of this decades-long evolution towards ever-higher levels of abstraction, ever closer to human intention. Each of these stages promised to make programming easier, faster, and more accessible. And each stage brought new challenges, new complexities, and required new ways of thinking and new skills.

What do we learn from this?

The evolution was relentless: ever-higher abstraction, ever closer to human intent. Vibe Coding is just the next logical step – but perhaps one where our co-pilot suddenly wants to take the controls.

Despite All Abstraction: Why the Basics (Still) Matter

Amidst all the enthusiasm for new abstractions – be it OOP, frameworks, or now AI – we must not forget one thing: the fundamentals. No matter how fancy the tool that generates code for us or takes work off our hands, in the end, this code runs on a real machine. And the laws of computer science still apply.

- **Algorithms & Data Structures:** Whether you write a loop yourself or the AI generates it – the choice of the right algorithm and the appropriate data structure determines performance and scalability. An AI might be able to write a sorting function, but does it also understand when Quicksort is better than Bubble Sort (hopefully always!) and why? You need to understand it to guide the AI correctly or evaluate its output.
- **Complexity (Big O):** How does the code behave under load? Is it $O(n)$, $O(n \log n)$, or even $O(n^2)$? An AI might spit out code that works for small amounts of data but explodes with large inputs.

Understanding time and space complexity remains essential for building performant systems.

- **Architectural Principles:** SOLID, KISS, DRY, Design Patterns – these principles are not ends in themselves. They help build maintainable, flexible, and robust systems. An AI might know about them, but does it apply them sensibly? Or does it just generate locally optimized code that causes problems in the overall picture? The ability to design and evaluate good architecture becomes even more important.

- **Debugging & Problem Solving:** Even with AI assistance – errors will always occur. The ability to systematically analyze problems, form hypotheses, and narrow down sources of error remains a core competency. You need to understand *why* something isn't working, not just *that* it isn't working.

The bottom line: Abstraction is good, ignorance is fatal. Even if the AI seems to work magic – the physics of bits and bytes still apply. Forgetting the fundamentals means building on sand, no matter how cool the "vibe" is.

The Tools of the New Magic: AI-Powered Editors & Platforms

Every new era needs its tools. For Vibe Coding, these are editors and platforms that don't just treat AI as an add-on, but as a core component. As of early 2025, several approaches were gaining traction:

- **AI-Native Editors:** Tools like **Cursor** emerged, essentially a fork of VS Code but deeply integrated with AI from the ground up. They allowed selecting code and giving natural language instructions ("Refactor this," "Add error handling," "Explain this regex"). These tools could analyze the entire codebase, reference specific files (@file) or documentation (@doc), and even operate in an "agent mode" to tackle tasks more autonomously.
- **Integrated IDE Assistants:** Established assistants like **GitHub Copilot** (powered by models like OpenAI's GPT-4) evolved beyond

simple code completion. They gained chat interfaces within the IDE, better context awareness, and more sophisticated code generation and debugging capabilities (e.g., Copilot Chat, Copilot Workspace previews). Similar features appeared in tools from Google (e.g., Gemini in Android Studio, IDX), JetBrains, and others.

- **Agentic Development Platforms:** Platforms like **Replit** (with its Replit AI features) aimed to provide an end-to-end experience, allowing users to build, test, and deploy entire applications, often using AI agents to handle significant parts of the workflow, all within a browser-based environment. Other players explored similar concepts, focusing on generating full-stack applications from high-level descriptions.

- **General Purpose LLMs:** Beyond specialized tools, general large language models like **OpenAI's ChatGPT (GPT-4 and beyond), Anthropic's Claude (e.g., Claude 3 family), and Google's Gemini** demonstrated increasingly powerful coding abilities, usable via chat interfaces or APIs for various coding tasks, from generation to explanation and debugging.

Open-source models also played a growing role. These types of tools are the catalysts. They make the abstract tangible, the "vibing" practically feasible. They aim to make us faster, free us from routine tasks, so we can focus on the creative, architectural aspects. Or so they promise.

In short: These new tools are more than just IDEs with AI features. They are the interface to a new programming reality – and they will fundamentally change the way we work, whether we like it or not.

Chapter 2: The Tide is Turning – Why This is More Than Just a Flash in the Pan

Okay, new buzzword, new tools. We've seen it all before. But why does it feel different this time? Why is everyone suddenly talking about it, from the hippest startups in Silicon Valley to established corporations? Has "Vibe Coding" really come to stay, or is it just the next entry in the graveyard of hyped technologies? Online discussions are heating up – oscillating between boundless optimism ("Finally, no more boilerplate!") and deep skepticism ("This can't possibly end well!"). It's time to weigh the arguments.

The Establishment Nods (Cautiously)

A strong indicator that something is more than just a fad: when the "big players" jump on board. And they

15

are. We hear from influential startup incubators like **Y Combinator** that a significant portion of their latest batch relies heavily on AI-generated code – not just for prototypes, but for their core products. The core message from YC and others, often echoed in talks and posts around early 2025, was essentially: "*Vibe Coding is the future*," because many of the most promising startups were already working this way. When the people betting on the next big thing put their money (and reputation) on the line, asserting that successful companies can be built with minimal teams and maximum AI leverage, people listen. This massive productivity gain, the ability to achieve more with fewer people, is naturally music to the ears of Venture Capital (VC) investors, further fueling the trend.

AI pioneers and thought leaders, like the aforementioned Andrej Karpathy, also see this not just as a neat gimmick, but as the *future* way of programming. When someone significantly involved in developing these technologies says, "This is the new normal," it carries weight.

This is about more than just code generation. It's a fundamental shift in how we communicate our intentions to machines. Away from rigid syntax, towards a more intuitive, natural language description of what we want to achieve. This aligns with a broader trend in human-computer interaction aimed at making technology more accessible and, well, more human.

The message is clear: When VCs and AI gurus are in the same boat shouting "Vibe Coding!", it's more than just ripples on the water. It's a strong indication that the tectonic plates of software development are shifting.

The Drivers: Speed, Baby, Speed! (And Accessibility)

Why is this catching on? Because it damn well works – at least for certain things – and solves real problems. The appeal stems from several sources:

- **Speed:** This is the most obvious point. The time it takes to get from an idea to a working prototype can be drastically reduced. Hours instead of days, days instead of weeks. Imagine discussing a new feature idea on Monday morning and having a clickable prototype cobbled together by the AI by the afternoon. This changes the game for innovation and experimentation. Repetitive tasks, boilerplate code, database setups, or implementing standard authentication flows – AI can often handle all this faster and (sometimes) with fewer errors.
- **Accessibility:** Suddenly, people who couldn't write a line of code before can build software. The subject matter expert who knows exactly

how a process needs to be optimized but previously depended on the IT department? The designer with a clear vision for a UI but lacking the skills to implement it? Vibe Coding dramatically lowers the barrier to entry. The "democratization" argument is strong here: potentially, anyone can become a software developer, at least for simpler applications.

- **Innovation & Productivity (even for us pros):** When AI takes over the routine jobs, we experienced developers have more time for the tricky stuff: the architecture, the complex algorithms, the truly novel ideas. It can boost creativity because experimentation becomes easier. You can quickly try something out without getting bogged down in implementation details for days. Productivity increases because we can focus on the *What* and *Why*, instead of just the *How*.

So why the hype? Faster, more accessible, more productive – the temptations are obvious. Vibe Coding hits a nerve in an industry addicted to efficiency. But like any powerful temptation, the question of risks and side effects arises...

The Secret Superpower: Ever Smarter LLMs

All of this would, of course, be just hot air without the rapid development of the underlying technology: Large Language Models (LLMs). The models behind tools like ChatGPT (GPT-4 and successors), Claude (like the Claude 3 family), Google's Gemini, and various open-source initiatives (like Llama, Mistral) are getting exponentially better at understanding and generating not only human language but also programming languages.

Previously, they might have completed a few code snippets. Today (as of early/mid-2025), they understand more complex instructions, can work across multiple files, consider the context of a project (sometimes with very large context windows), and generate code that goes far beyond simple boilerplate. They learn abstractions, recognize intentions, and can even assist significantly in debugging and explaining code.

Development continues towards multimodal models that can understand not only text but also images (e.g., UI sketches) or even spoken language as input.

Imagine sketching a wireframe on a tablet and saying, "Turn this into a React component," and the AI delivers the code. This is rapidly moving from science fiction to reality.

Of course, it's not perfect yet. AI still hallucinates (makes things up), produces subtle errors, or writes code that works but is inefficient or hard to maintain. But the progress curve remains incredibly steep.

The key factor: Without the exploding capabilities of LLMs, Vibe Coding would have remained a pipe dream. Their learning curve is the fuel for this potential revolution – and it shows no signs of slowing down so far.

Chapter 3: The Art of the Prompt – How to Tango with AI

Okay, so the AI can write code. Great. But how do we get it to write *the right* code? Just muttering "Make me an app" won't cut it (yet). This is where the new core competency comes into play: Prompt Engineering. Or as I like to call it: Teaching the AI what we *really* want without it getting offended or building complete nonsense. It's less witchcraft than you might think, but it requires a new way of communicating.

From Command Receiver to Conversation Partner

Interacting with these new AI tools feels different from traditional programming. It's less of a dictation and more of a dialogue, an iterative approach to the solution:

- **Natural Language is Key:** You describe what you need, often in simple, direct language. "Create a function that takes a list of user objects and returns it sorted by age." Some tools even allow voice input. This makes it more intuitive, lowers the barrier, and sometimes almost feels like a conversation.

- **Iteration is King:** Rarely does the AI deliver the perfect result on the first try. The initial output is often just a starting point, a rough draft. You look at the generated code and provide feedback: "That's good, but please use arrow functions." or "Error handling is still missing." or "Can you make this more performant?". It's a back-and-forth, a refinement process, similar to a code review with a human colleague, except the colleague is infinitely patient and never gets tired (and rarely argues back).

- **Context, Context, Context:** The better tools can understand the context of your project. You can point them to specific files, code sections, or even external documentation (often using special syntax like @file or @doc). "Look at UserService.java and implement the new method based on the pattern there." The more context you provide – about the existing code, the architecture, the libraries used – the more relevant and accurate the AI's output will be.

- **Fast Editing Loops:** Many AI editors offer features to edit code directly via prompt. Select, press a shortcut, give an instruction ("Convert this to a try-catch block"), done. This vastly speeds up small changes and refactorings, making the iterative process smoother.

What this means for us: Just barking commands at the AI isn't enough. Successful "vibing" is a tango – an iterative dance of precise instruction, critical review, and targeted feedback. Prompting becomes the new, indispensable core competency.

Practical Tips for Better Prompts

So, prompting well is crucial. But how do you do it effectively? Here are a few tips that have proven useful in practice for steering the AI more effectively:

1. **Be Specific, Not Vague:** Instead of "Make the database query faster," try "Optimize this SQL query for PostgreSQL. Add an index to the 'created_at' column and use a prepared

statement." The more precise the instruction, the better the result. Vague prompts lead to vague (and often useless) outcomes.

2. **Provide Context:** Refer to relevant files, code snippets, or even external documentation. "Implement authentication using JWT, based on the example in auth_service.py and the documentation at [Link]." Many tools allow embedding code or file references directly in the prompt. The more the AI knows about the "where" and "why," the better the generated code will fit.

3. **Define the "What," Not Just the "How":** Clearly describe the desired outcome or behavior. "Create a React component that displays a list of products. Each product should have a name, price, and image. Clicking on a product should open the detail page." However, sometimes specifying the "how" is also helpful if a particular approach needs to be followed.

4. **Request a Specific Format or Style:** "Generate the code as a Python class.", "Use functional

programming.", "Write comments for each method.", "Adhere to the PEP 8 style guide." This helps maintain consistency in the codebase.

5. **Use "Personas":** Sometimes assigning a role to the AI helps influence the output. "Respond like an experienced security expert: What vulnerabilities do you see in this code?" or "Explain this concept to me like I'm five." This can guide the focus and level of detail in the response.

6. **Set Clear Constraints and Assumptions:** "Use only standard libraries.", "Assume the input is always valid JSON.", "The function should take no more than 100ms." This avoids unexpected dependencies or misbehavior with invalid inputs.

7. **Provide Examples (Few-Shot Prompting):** If you want a specific pattern or format, include one or two examples directly in the prompt. "Convert the following data to JSON format: Input: 'Name: Max, Age: 30'; Output: {'name': 'Max', 'age': 30}. Input: 'Name: Anna, Age: 25'; Output: ?" AI often learns very well from

examples.

8. **Iterate and Refine:** The first prompt is rarely perfect. Use the AI's response, identify weaknesses, and ask follow-up questions to improve the result. "That's good, but can you add input validation?" or "The code throws an exception if the list is empty. Please fix it."

Remember: Prompting isn't an exact science; it requires practice and a willingness to experiment. It's a dialogue where you need to learn how the specific AI "thinks" and how best to guide it towards the desired results.

Vibe Coding in Action: What Can It (Supposedly) Do?

Okay, enough theory. Where is this approach already being used? The use cases are diverse, ranging from small helpers to ambitious projects:

- **Rapid Prototyping:** This is the prime use case. Have an app idea? Describe the core features, let the AI build a basic structure. In hours instead of days, you have something tangible to gather feedback or convince investors. Example: A simple event management app with a calendar view and registration – maybe not perfect, but quickly available.

- **Automation of Routine Tasks:** Database setups, generating CRUD operations, building interfaces to standard APIs, writing boilerplate for tests – all tasks that are important but rarely fun. AI can take a lot of this work off your hands. "Generate the SQL DDL for this user table with indexes on name and email."

- **Websites and Simple UIs:** "Create a landing page for me with a hero section, three feature boxes, and a contact form. Use Tailwind CSS." For standard websites or internal tools, this can work surprisingly well.

- **Data Analysis and Scripting:** "Write a Python script that reads this CSV, aggregates sales by region, and plots a bar chart." For data wrangling and small automation scripts, AI is often very helpful.

- **Learning and Understanding:** "Explain this code snippet." or "Show me an example of the Strategy Pattern in C#." AI tools can also serve as patient tutors for learning new languages, frameworks, or concepts.
- **"Software for One Person":** Small, custom tools for personal use that you might never have built otherwise because the effort was too great. A script that automatically generates reports, a small tool to manage a personal library...

The point is: From quick prototypes to small, custom helpers – the applications are real and varied. Vibe Coding isn't a Swiss Army knife for every problem, but for certain tasks, it's a damn useful tool in the toolbox.

The Turbo Boost: Show Me the Numbers!

This all sounds nice, but does it really deliver? The numbers and reports we're hearing are sometimes impressive:

- **Massive Time Savings:** Projects that traditionally would have taken weeks are completed in days. Prototypes emerge in hours. Some report up to 10x speed improvements for specific tasks.

- **Smaller Teams, Big Impact:** Startups heavily relying on Vibe Coding are reportedly achieving significant results and revenue with tiny core teams (sometimes just 1-2 developers directing the AI). This challenges traditional notions of team size and scaling.

- **Increased Developer Productivity:** Studies (though always to be taken with a grain of salt) suggest that developers using AI tools complete tasks significantly faster and feel more productive. They can achieve more in less time or have more time for complex problems.

Of course, these are often optimistic figures from the honeymoon phase. The long-term costs of maintenance or fixing subtle AI errors aren't factored in yet. But the short-term productivity boost seems real.

What do the numbers say? The stopwatch doesn't lie: In the short term, Vibe Coding appears to offer a tremendous speed advantage. Whether this rush is sustainable or ends in the inevitable maintenance hangover, however, is the million-dollar question.

Chapter 4: A World of Possibilities – A Coder's Paradise?

Now that we've clarified what Vibe Coding is and why it might be more than just hot air, let's dive into the bright side. What can we actually do with it? Where are the opportunities that might even make us a bit envious of the next generation of developers (or give us new superpowers ourselves)? A world beckons where ideas become reality faster and routine work belongs to the past. But is it really paradise?

Prototyping on Steroids: Bringing Ideas to Life Before the Coffee Gets Cold

We've touched on this, but it's so central that we need to emphasize it again: Rapid Prototyping. As an experienced software professional, you know the dilemma: A brilliant idea needs to be visualized quickly to get stakeholders on board, test assumptions, or simply see if it has wings. In the past, this often meant drawing wireframes, clicking through mockups, maybe building a few static HTML pages – a process that could take days or weeks.

With Vibe Coding, you could potentially say: "Give me an app with user login via Google, a dashboard view with three widgets (user stats, recent activities, open tasks), and a table to display customer data from a Firestore collection. Use React and Tailwind CSS. Use fake data for the widgets." The AI gets to work and spits out – ideally – a first, functional draft. This is invaluable in the early stages of a project.

- **Validate Faster:** You can test hypotheses about features or entire products in the market or with test users at lightning speed. Does the idea work? Do users understand the flow? Is the feature even useful? Feedback comes earlier, reducing the risk of costly misdevelopments.

- **Cost-Effective Experiments:** Trying out a crazy idea that previously never had the budget or time? Today, it might be just a few well-formulated prompts away. This significantly lowers the barrier to innovation. Failing is cheaper, so hopefully, more risks are taken.

- **MVPs in No Time:** Startups or new product lines quickly need a Minimum Viable Product (MVP) to attract initial users and get real market feedback. Vibe Coding can help get this MVP up and running extremely fast, drastically shortening the time-to-market.

The Superpower: Validating ideas before the investor gets impatient? Building MVPs while the competition is still planning? This is where Vibe Coding plays to its strengths and has the potential to radically accelerate the innovation cycle.

The Democratization of Creation: Everyone Becomes a Developer (Oh God!)

This is perhaps the aspect making the biggest waves – and possibly causing the most worry lines for us old hands. If everyone can build software with voice commands, what happens to our profession? But let's first look at the positive side, the utopian potential:

- **Empowerment for Non-Programmers:** Imagine

the marketing manager building a small tool themselves to analyze campaign data without waiting for the overloaded IT department. Or the biologist creating a script to evaluate complex experimental data tailored exactly to their needs. Or the teacher generating a simple learning app for their class to teach specific material. People with subject matter expertise but without traditional programming skills can suddenly create solutions for their own problems. This unlocks a huge reservoir of creativity and specific knowledge that previously remained untapped.

- **"Software for One Person" Becomes Reality:** We all have those small, annoying tasks in everyday life that could be automated if only we had the time (and sometimes the inclination) to write a script for them. With Vibe Coding, it becomes conceivable that everyone can "vibe" together their own small, custom helpers – from a personal finance tracker to an automated vacation planner.

- **Broader Participation in Digital Design:**

Software shapes our world to an ever-increasing extent. If more people – not just professional coders – can participate in its design, it could lead to more diverse, inclusive, and needs-based solutions. Niches could be served that are uninteresting for large software companies, and local communities could develop their own digital tools.

The Grand Vision (or Danger?): The power of software creation for everyone? Vibe Coding tears down walls and could spawn legions of new "developers." A fascinating, but admittedly also slightly frightening prospect, especially when considering the potential quality and security of this "democratically" created software.

Productivity Boost for Pros: More Time for What Matters

Okay, what's in it for us, who already know how to write code? Are we now being relegated to mere prompt managers, just feeding the AI? Not necessarily. Used correctly, Vibe Coding can also be a powerful tool for experienced developers and technical leads, complementing rather than replacing us:

- **Offload the Drudgery:** Writing boilerplate code, integrating standard libraries, creating configuration files, generating simple unit tests, implementing CRUD interfaces – all these repetitive, often boring tasks can be taken over by the AI. This frees up mental space and reduces the "copy-paste" portion of our work.

- **Focus on Architecture and Complexity:** If we spend less time typing routine code, we have more time and cognitive capacity for the big picture: designing robust and scalable systems, defining clear interfaces, ensuring non-functional requirements (performance, security, reliability), solving truly complex algorithmic or logical problems. Exactly the things we, as experienced professionals, are actually paid for and that require our expertise.

- **Faster Learning & Experimentation:** Trying out a new technology, a new framework, or an unfamiliar architectural pattern? AI can act as a personal, patient tutor, providing code examples, explaining concepts, and generating initial implementation attempts. This significantly accelerates onboarding in new projects or technologies.

- **The "Super-Junior" by Your Side:** Imagine having an extremely fast, tireless junior developer you can delegate clearly defined tasks to. They might not get everything perfect and need supervision, but they deliver results quickly that you can then review, adapt, and refine. Collaboration with a good code AI can feel similar – if you learn how to lead it correctly.

The Opportunity for Pros: No need to fear unemployment (for now)! Vibe Coding is less a replacement and more a potential upgrade – the chance to delegate routine tasks and finally focus fully on the truly tricky architectural puzzles and strategic decisions.

Unleashing Creativity: When Programming Becomes Play?

Can typing prompts actually be creative? Perhaps even more so than classic programming, which is often dominated by the constraints of syntax and implementation details? Some arguments support this:

- **Fewer Syntax Hurdles, More Idea Flow:** Sometimes the rigid syntax of a programming language or the complexity of a framework blocks the creative flow. Being able to focus more on describing the idea, the desired behavior, or the goal, instead of worrying about correct bracketing or the right API method, can be liberating and encourage the flow of ideas.

- **Playful Experimentation Made Easy:** The ease with which variants can be generated and tested invites play and experimentation. "What happens if I replace this algorithm with another one?", "What does the UI look like with a dark theme?", "Generate three different approaches for this function." AI becomes a tireless partner in brainstorming and trying out alternatives, which can lead to surprising results.

- **Discovering New Solutions:** Sometimes the AI suggests solutions or uses libraries you wouldn't have thought of yourself – perhaps because it knows an obscure but fitting library, suggests an elegant pattern, or simply follows a different "thought" process based on the vast amounts of data it was trained on. This can broaden one's horizons and lead to better or at least different solutions.

- **Emotional Connection and Flow?** Some proponents even speak of Vibe Coding fostering a more "emotional connection" to the work because it feels more like self-expression than dryly typing code. Well, that's debatable, but the much-cited "flow state" might indeed be easier to achieve due to the faster feedback loop and the feeling of interacting directly with ideas.

The Creative Spark: Less syntax frustration, more room for ideas? Vibe Coding could actually make programming more playful, intuitive, and experimental, helping us find solutions that lie beyond the beaten path – provided we use it as a springboard for creativity and not a substitute for it.

Chapter 5: Shadows on the Horizon – The Dark Side of the Vibe

Okay, enough praise and talk of the brave new world. Every powerful technology has its downsides, and with something as potentially disruptive as Vibe Coding, the pitfalls are particularly deep and numerous. Remember the quote "forgetting that the code even exists"? Sounds cool and like maximum abstraction, but it might just be the most direct path to maintenance hell, security disasters, and the loss of our core competencies. So, let's buckle up; it's going to get uncomfortable. It's time to soberly examine the risks.

Pandora's Box: Code Without Understanding

This is the biggest, brightest red warning light flashing over the whole topic of Vibe Coding. The AI spits out code, it seems to work (at least at first glance, in the happy path), so it gets copy-pasted and integrated into the project. But does the developer who entered the prompt *really* understand what this code does? In detail? With all its side effects?

- **Large-Scale Black-Box Programming:** When we use code whose internal logic we don't grasp or don't bother to understand, we're building on sand. What happens in unexpected inputs or edge cases? How does this opaque block of code interact with other parts of the system under load? What if an underlying assumption made by the AI (based on its training data) turns out to be wrong in our specific context? We create dependencies we cannot control.

- **Debugging Becomes a Nightmare:** Finding a bug in code you wrote yourself (and hopefully understood and documented) is hard enough. But hunting a bug in complex, perhaps sub-optimally structured, AI-generated code that you only superficially know? Good luck with that. It's like archaeology without a map in a labyrinth of alien thought patterns. The time saved during writing is often paid back double or triple during debugging.

- **Subtle Errors and Insidious Security Flaws:** AI models are trained to recognize patterns and generate code that often *works*. But they have no real understanding of security, robustness, efficiency, or the long-term implications of their code. They can unintentionally introduce common vulnerabilities (like SQL injection, cross-site scripting, insecure defaults), create race conditions, or simply write terribly inefficient code that collapses under load or consumes unnecessary resources.

- **Quality Lottery Instead of Engineering:** The quality of AI-generated code can vary wildly – depending on the model, the prompt, the context, and often just chance. Sometimes the result is surprisingly elegant and correct, other times it's hair-raising junk that compiles but contains logical errors or violates all best practices. Relying on it blindly is a gamble – the exact opposite of what professional software development should be: a disciplined engineering effort.

The hard truth: Adopting code you don't understand?

That's like driving blindfolded, relying solely on a GPS that might have outdated maps. Sooner or later, you're going to crash – guaranteed. And then you'll be standing there, not even knowing how to deploy the airbag.

Maintainability? Scalability? Uh... *Vibes*?

Software is rarely a one-off product. It lives, it changes, it needs to be adapted, extended, corrected, and often scaled. And precisely here, in the lifecycle after the initial creation, the "vibe" approach could reveal its Achilles' heel and cost us dearly.

- **Spaghetti Code on Autopilot:** When code emerges organically from prompts ("Do this," "Add that," "Change this"), without a clear, overarching architectural vision enforced by an experienced human, chaos quickly looms. The AI might optimize brilliantly for the individual prompt but easily lose sight of the big picture. The result can be an unstructured, hard-to-follow lump of code, full of hidden dependencies and inconsistent patterns – the nightmare of every maintenance team (and your future self).

- **The Challenge of Updates and Refactoring:** How do you update an application whose codebase you only partially understand and which might lack a clear, comprehensible structure? Changes in one place can have unpredictable effects elsewhere. Refactoring such code to improve it or adapt it to new requirements becomes extremely risky, time-consuming, and error-prone.

- **Scaling Problems Pre-Programmed:** Was the application built with scalability and performance in mind? Did the AI choose efficient algorithms and data structures, or did it just grab the first solution that worked for the moment? Applications quickly "vibed" together often hit painful limits when user numbers increase, data volumes grow, or requirements become more complex. Retrofitting for scalability is then often disproportionately expensive and difficult.

- **Technical Debt with Compound Interest:** Every shortcut in design, every misunderstood code block, every piece of missing documentation (because "the AI knows what it's doing" or "I can just ask it later") is technical debt. With unreflective Vibe Coding, there's an acute danger of accumulating this debt at record speed. And just like real debt, interest will eventually come due – in the form of longer development times, higher error rates, and soaring maintenance costs that can quickly eat up any initial speed advantages.

The long-term bill: Built fast, rots fast? Without discipline, human foresight, and solid architecture, vibe code threatens to become a ticking time bomb of technical debt that will blow up in our faces later and stifle innovation.

The "I Don't Understand Anything" Developer: Are We Unlearning the Craft?

What happens to us developers – and especially the next generation – if we rely too heavily on the convenience of AI? If "vibing" replaces the arduous but necessary process of learning and understanding concepts?

- **Erosion of Core Competencies:** If you never implement algorithms yourself, design data structures from scratch, or systematically analyze complex errors because the AI (seemingly) handles it – how are you supposed to develop or even maintain these fundamental skills? Isn't there a danger that we'll unlearn the actual craft of programming, problem-solving, and structured thinking, becoming mere operators?

- **Critical Dependence on the Tool:** What happens if the preferred AI tool goes down, changes its API, suddenly costs money, or simply can't generate a good solution for a specific, new problem? Developers who rely too heavily on AI and no longer master the basics could suddenly find themselves helpless when they need to work "manually" again or solve a problem beyond the AI's comfort zone.

- **Less Rigorous Problem Solving and**

Creativity: Grappling with a difficult problem, trying out different (and sometimes wrong) approaches, diving deep into the subject matter – all this is often a painful but incredibly important part of the learning process. It leads to deeper understanding and often to truly creative, unexpected solutions. If the AI always provides an (apparent) solution immediately, this crucial step of "productive struggle" might be skipped. Does this really foster creativity or just the ability to accept the first available answer?

- **The Dangerous Illusion of Competence:** Vibe Coding can quickly give you the feeling of being extremely productive and building complex things, even if you're actually just a good "AI whisperer" skillfully operating the machine. This can lead to dangerous overconfidence, especially when it comes to judging the quality, reliability, and long-term viability of the generated code. You *feel* competent without perhaps truly *being* competent.

The danger of convenience: Anyone who only pushes buttons forgets the craft. The temptation to outsource the strenuous work of thinking and understanding to the AI could degrade us into mere tool operators, helpless when the supposed "magic" fails or deeper understanding is required.

Security in the Age of Vibe Coding: A Minefield?

As if all that weren't enough, there's another particularly tricky point that should give us technical leaders sleepless nights: security. AI-generated code isn't inherently insecure, but the Vibe Coding process, especially when done unreflectively, carries specific and sometimes new risks:

1. **Insecure Defaults and Outdated Patterns:** AI models learn from vast amounts of code from the internet, including a lot of old, insecure code or code using outdated libraries and insecure practices. If you don't explicitly request secure practices, the AI might unintentionally choose insecure defaults or reproduce known

vulnerability patterns simply because they were common in the training data.

2. **Amplification of Vulnerability Patterns:** If certain vulnerability patterns (e.g., SQL injection vulnerabilities in older PHP code, missing input validation in web frameworks) are frequent in the training data, the AI might unintentionally reproduce and even amplify these patterns because it recognizes them as "typical" or "probable."

3. **AI's Lack of Real Security Understanding:** The AI has no inherent understanding of security concepts, threat models, or attack vectors. It optimizes for functional code that matches the prompt, not necessarily for robust and secure code. It won't proactively think about input validation, proper output encoding, or the principle of least privilege unless explicitly prompted to do so in detail.

4. **Risk of "Prompt Injection":** In more complex systems, especially where user input or external data could become part of prompts (e.g., generating dynamic queries or scripts), there's a

real danger of prompt injection. An attacker could try to manipulate the prompt to make the AI perform undesired actions, leak sensitive data, or generate insecure code.

5. **Secrets in Prompts – The Absolute Taboo:** Developers might be tempted to put API keys, passwords, or other sensitive information directly into prompts to give the AI context ("Connect to this database..."). This is an absolute no-go! These prompts are often logged by providers, used to improve models, or could be otherwise compromised. Secrets *never* belong in prompts but must be managed through secure mechanisms.

6. **Unvetted Dependencies:** The AI might suggest using certain libraries or packages without checking their security status, known vulnerabilities (CVEs), or the trustworthiness of the source. Blindly accepting dependencies is always risky, but it's especially dangerous with AI-generated code where you didn't make the selection yourself.

Practical Security Tips for Vibe Coding:

- **Never put secrets in prompts!** Use established methods for managing secrets (secrets managers, environment variables, configuration files outside the codebase).

- *Rigorously validate all inputs and outputs:* Treat AI-generated code like any other code – trust no external input and carefully validate and/or encode all outputs, especially when used in security-critical contexts (e.g., generating SQL queries, HTML output, file system access). Sanitize early, escape late!

- **Explicitly request security (and be specific):** Prompt things like "Write secure code," "Implement input validation against XSS and SQL injection for all user inputs," "Use parameterized queries for all database access," "Use modern and secure cryptography libraries for...".

- **Code review is mandatory (with a security focus):** *All* AI-generated code, especially if security-relevant, must be reviewed by an experienced human, ideally with an explicit focus on security. Use checklists (e.g., OWASP Top 10) and static application security testing (SAST) tools that can also check AI-generated code.

- **Scan dependencies:** Use Software Composition Analysis (SCA) tools to ensure no known vulnerabilities lurk in the libraries suggested or used by the AI. Keep dependencies up to date.
- **Apply the Principle of Least Privilege:** Ensure the generated code and the environment it runs in only have the permissions absolutely necessary to perform their task.

The security mantra: The AI as a security expert? Forget it. At best, it's an assistant that can point out known patterns. Without explicit security requirements in the prompt, human oversight, rigorous testing, and established security practices throughout the development process, AI-generated code is an uncalculated risk. Security remains manual labor and, above all, brain work.

Chapter 6: The Next Generation in Limbo – Education in the AI Era

The way we develop software is changing rapidly. But what does this mean for those just starting out? How do you educate developers in an age where AI can generate code at the push of a button? This is one of the trickiest questions facing universities, bootcamps, and companies. And it affects us seasoned veterans too: How do we stay relevant, and how do we train the next generation who will eventually maintain our complex systems? The answer will partly determine the future of our industry.

From Theory to Practice to Bootcamp: The Evolution of Developer Education

Developer education was constantly evolving even before the AI revolution, always trying to keep pace with rapid technological development. Let's recall the stages:

- **The Academic Beginnings:** Computer science at universities used to be very theoretical. The focus was on mathematics, algorithm theory, formal languages, and compiler construction. Practical software development was sometimes secondary or limited to small exercises. You learned the fundamentals, but not necessarily how to build a modern, complex web application in a team using the latest frameworks.

- **The Call for Practical Relevance:** With the boom of the IT industry and the growing demand for developers who could be productive immediately in projects, pressure mounted on universities. They responded (sometimes faster, sometimes slower) with more practice-oriented curricula, more project work, internships, and industry collaborations. The focus shifted more towards specific programming languages, databases, frameworks, and tools that were in demand in the market.

- **The Rise of Bootcamps:** In response to the

persistent skills shortage and the perceived inertia of traditional multi-year degree programs, coding bootcamps sprang up like mushrooms. Their promise: From beginner to "job-ready" web developer (or data scientist, etc.) in just a few intensive months. The approach: Extremely practical, focused on currently in-demand technologies and methods, often with direct connections to potential employers. A controversial, but for many, also successful model for quickly entering the industry.

- **Online Learning for Everyone:** Platforms like Coursera, edX, Udemy, Pluralsight, as well as free resources like YouTube channels and blogs, revolutionized access to learning materials. Anyone with an internet connection could (and can) acquire knowledge on almost any conceivable tech topic, often at high quality and low cost, or even for free. Self-study and continuous learning became a crucial pillar of competence development.

Into this already dynamic and diverse educational landscape, AI now bursts in with its code-generating capabilities, potentially turning everything upside down.

Vibe Coding in the Lecture Hall: Accelerator or Brake?

The new AI tools offer tempting possibilities for education, but they also harbor significant dangers and didactic challenges:

- **The Turbo-Learner? The Promise:** AI can act as a tireless, patient tutor. It can explain code ("What exactly does this function do?"), point out errors ("Why isn't my code working?"), generate examples for concepts or patterns ("Show me the Strategy Pattern in Python."), help with syntax ("What was the syntax for a lambda expression again?"). This can potentially flatten the often frustrating initial learning curve, especially with picky syntax details, and significantly accelerate learning. Students could explore new technologies and concepts faster and focus on understanding the logic.

- **The Danger of Superficiality: The Curse?** But if the AI always provides the solution immediately, where is the actual learning effect? The arduous struggle with a problem, the hours spent debugging, the "Why the hell isn't this working?" – all this is often painful but essential for developing a deep, intuitive understanding of the material, for learning problem-solving strategies, and for learning from mistakes. Is there an acute danger that students will only learn to operate the AI skillfully ("prompt jockeys") but no longer learn to analyze problems independently, find creative solutions, and understand code from the ground up? Will critical thinking be replaced by "prompting and copying" without truly internalizing the underlying concepts?

- **The Shrinking Knowledge Gap – or Growing Illusion?** Vibe Coding seemingly lowers the technical barrier to entry drastically. On the one hand, this is good because it gives more people access to software development and might attract talents who wouldn't have dared before.

On the other hand, it could lead to graduates entering the market who can quickly "vibe" together prototypes but have no clue about the fundamental concepts of computer science, algorithms, data structures, or system architecture. They might develop a dangerous illusion of competence that shatters the moment they encounter more complex problems or need to maintain and extend existing code.

The didactic dilemma: The AI tutor – brilliant learning accelerator or dangerous crutch that prevents learning to walk? Education faces the enormous challenge of teaching the use of these powerful tools without sacrificing critical thinking, problem-solving skills, and a solid foundation of knowledge and understanding. New teaching methods and assessment formats are urgently needed.

The Chicken-and-Egg Problem: No Juniors, No Seniors?

One of the biggest concerns hotly debated in the developer community and by companies: What happens to entry-level positions, the junior developer jobs?

- **Automation of Entry-Level Tasks:** Many typical tasks traditionally assigned to beginners – simple bug fixes, writing boilerplate code, implementing simple features according to clear specifications, creating basic unit tests – are precisely the things where AI tools already shine or soon will. If companies can increasingly automate these tasks, the question arises: Do they still need as many juniors? Will the demand for entry-level developers decrease?

- **The Missing Experience Loop:** Traditionally, juniors learn "on the job." They start with simpler tasks, make mistakes (which are hopefully caught by experienced colleagues), learn from code reviews, observe the seniors, and thus gradually grow into more complex tasks and greater responsibility. If these entry-level opportunities and learning situations disappear or are significantly reduced, how are future senior developers and architects supposed to gain the necessary practical experience and deep system understanding? Where will the next generation of experts come from if the first crucial step on the career ladder is missing or looks completely different?

- **Shifting Roles – An Opportunity?** Some argue more optimistically: Perhaps the roles will simply shift. Maybe fewer pure "junior coders" will be needed, while seniors focus more on reviewing AI code, defining architecture, solving complex problems, and strategically directing the AI. Others hope that AI tools will actually support juniors, helping them learn faster and become more productive, perhaps even allowing them to take on more demanding tasks earlier, thus steepening the overall learning curve.

- **Mentoring in Danger:** An important aspect of starting a career is mentoring by more experienced colleagues. If fewer juniors are hired, or if they primarily interact with AI tools and seemingly need less guidance, important mentoring relationships and the informal transfer of knowledge from experienced to young developers could suffer. This could not only slow down individual development but also hinder the transmission of implicit knowledge and best practices within teams.

The future question: If AI eats the entry-level jobs, who will mature into experienced seniors? The chicken-and-egg problem of the AI era is real and poses a serious threat to the sustainable talent pipeline of the software industry. Companies and educational institutions urgently need to find new ways for juniors to gain valuable practical experience and be effectively nurtured in the age of AI.

The Skills of Tomorrow: What Do Developers Really Need to Know?

If AI takes over more and more of the actual typing, what skills will truly make the difference in the future? The role of the software developer is definitely changing – away from being purely a code producer towards something else, something more multi-dimensional. But what exactly?

- **Prompt Engineering as a Basic Skill:** Clearly, the ability to communicate effectively with AI will be central. This means formulating precise requirements, providing relevant context, steering the AI purposefully, and interpreting its responses. This is more than just asking questions; it's a form of requirements specification and control.

- **Critical Thinking & Evaluation Skills:** Even more important than prompting will be the ability to critically question and evaluate the AI's output. Does the code really work correctly and under all conditions? Is it implemented securely? Is it efficient enough? Is it maintainable and understandable? Does it meet the actual (often implicit) requirements? One must be able to assess the AI's suggestions like the code of a human colleague and make informed decisions about what to adopt, what to adapt, and what to discard.

- **Systems Thinking & Architectural Skills:** Understanding the big picture, designing robust, scalable, and maintainable systems, selecting the right technologies, patterns, and architectures – these skills become massively more valuable when the pure implementation details at the component level can be partially automated. The architect or senior developer who oversees the entire system and makes the strategic decisions becomes even more crucial.

- **Abstract Problem-Solving Skills:** The ability to analyze complex problems, break them down into smaller, manageable parts, develop and weigh different solution approaches remains absolutely essential – regardless of whether you write the code yourself in the end or guide the AI during implementation. The core work of software engineering is problem-solving, not typing.

- **Domain Knowledge & Requirements Analysis:** Understanding the subject area in which the software is used (finance, medicine, logistics, etc.) becomes more important. Developers need to deeply understand user problems and needs to formulate the right requirements and use AI meaningfully. The bridge between the business domain and technology becomes critical.

- **Collaboration (Human & AI):** Teamwork remains important, but it now also includes effective collaboration with AI assistants as part of the "team." One needs to know when to use AI best, how to leverage its strengths (e.g., for research, code generation, refactoring), and where its limitations and potential weaknesses lie.

- **Learnability & Adaptability:** The field is currently evolving so rapidly that the willingness and ability to continuously learn new things and adapt quickly to new tools, models, and paradigms might become the most important overarching trait of all. Those who stand still will be left behind.

The new job profile: Less typing, more thinking! The future belongs to developers and architects who can not only have code generated but also understand complex systems, critically evaluate, direct wisely, communicate effectively, and, above all, constantly evolve. The fundamentals of computer science and software engineering do not become obsolete but form the necessary foundation for these higher-value activities

.

Table: Evolving Developer Skills in the AI Era

Traditional Focus	Future / Increased Focus in AI Era	Required Skills
Manual Code Writing	Guiding AI, Steering Code Generation	Prompt Engineering, Understanding AI Capabilities & Limits
Syntax Mastery	Understanding Concepts, Evaluating Code Quality	Fundamental Programming Knowledge, Critical Thinking, Quality Awareness
Algorithm Implementation	Selecting, Adapting & Evaluating (AI-generated) Algorithms	Algorithm & Data Structure Knowledge, Performance Analysis
Detail-Oriented Debugging	Systemic Debugging, Analyzing Complex Errors (incl. in AI code)	Analytical Skills, System Understanding, Debugging Strategies
Focus on Individual Tasks	Systems Thinking, Architecture, Integration	Architectural Design, Interface Management, Understanding Non-Functional Requirements
Primarily	Technical Skills +	Effective Communication

Technical Skills	Communication, Collaboration & Domain Skills	(Human/AI), Teamwork, Domain Knowledge, Requirements Analysis
Learning Specific Technologies	Continuous Learning, Rapid Adaptation to New Tools & Paradigms	Learnability, Curiosity, Adaptability, Meta-Learning
-	Ethical Evaluation & Responsible AI Use	Ethical Awareness, Understanding Bias, Security & Privacy

Chapter 7: Charting the Course Forward – Responsible Vibing Instead of Blind Trust

Okay, we've explored the bright promises and dark abysses of Vibe Coding. The opportunities are tempting, the risks real. The question now is: How do we harness the enormous potential of this technology without plunging ourselves (and our projects) into ruin? Simply closing our eyes and hoping for the best is not an option for professional software developers and architects. Neither is completely demonizing the technology and ignoring the productivity gains. We need strategies, guardrails, and a healthy dose of common engineering sense to navigate this transformation responsibly. It's about understanding AI as what it is: an incredibly powerful tool, but just a tool – not a magical black box we can blindly trust.

Strategies Against Chaos: Guardrails for AI

If we want to prevent Vibe Coding from turning into a nightmare of technical debt, security vulnerabilities, and unmaintainable code, we need clear rules, established processes, and technical safeguards:

- **Rigorous Code Reviews (with Human Brains and Focus):** This is non-negotiable and arguably becomes even more critical. *Every* piece of AI-generated code integrated into the production base must be reviewed by an experienced human. This isn't just about whether the code is syntactically correct and *somehow* works, but primarily about readability, maintainability, efficiency, security, robustness, and adherence to architectural guidelines and coding standards. The four-eyes principle (or more) is essential here. Reviews might even need to be more intensive, as the "thoughts" of the AI "author" cannot be directly inferred.
- **Clear Quality Guidelines and Coding**

Standards: Teams must explicitly define and document what "good code" means in their context – even, and especially, if it comes from an AI. This includes naming conventions, commenting rules, preferred design patterns, but also performance targets, security requirements, and guidelines for dependency management. These standards must be actively enforced (e.g., through linters, static analysis) and checked in code reviews.

- **Architecture First, AI Second:** Before the AI starts generating, there needs to be a clear architectural vision designed and communicated by humans. Where are the module boundaries? What do the interfaces look like? What are the non-functional requirements (scalability, resilience, etc.)? Which technologies and patterns should be used? The AI can then help with the implementation *within* this framework, but the strategic, structural decisions must be made and enforced by experienced architects.

- **Automated Quality Assurance as a Safety Net:** Static Application Security Testing (SAST) to detect patterns and potential errors, Dynamic Application Security Testing (DAST) for runtime checks, comprehensive unit tests, integration tests, end-to-end tests, and performance tests – all these established QA tools are also (or especially) indispensable for AI-generated code. They provide a crucial safety net to detect errors and vulnerabilities early that might slip past a human reviewer. You can even ask the AI to generate tests for its own code – but these tests, too, must be carefully reviewed and supplemented!

- **Continuous Refactoring as Hygiene:** Technical debt always creeps in, potentially even faster with AI-generated code. Regular, planned refactoring to maintain code quality, improve structure, and reduce complexity is even more important in AI-assisted development. AI can also support this (e.g., with suggestions for simplification), but the initiative, evaluation, and execution of the refactoring must lie with the human team.

The motto: Wild West vibing leads to ruin. Only with

clear rules, strict reviews, and solid engineering practices can we tame the AI and use its power safely, sustainably, and responsibly.

Keeping Humans in the Loop: Oversight, Review, and Testing

The temptation is great to just hand over the controls to the AI and switch to autopilot. But that would be fatal, at least with the current state of technology. The "Human-in-the-Loop" approach – meaning constant involvement and control by humans – is crucial for responsible and successful Vibe Coding:

- **AI as Assistant, Not Replacement:** View the AI as an extremely fast, but sometimes somewhat naive or context-blind, junior developer, or as a very powerful tool like an advanced compiler or an extremely good search engine. It can make suggestions, generate code, handle routine tasks, provide knowledge – but the ultimate responsibility for the design, quality, and behavior of the final product always lies with the human developer or architect.

- **Understand Before Accepting:** This cannot be stressed enough: Never accept AI-generated code that you don't understand down to the details. Take the time to grasp the logic, question the AI's assumptions, consider potential side effects, and check if the code truly solves the problem rather than just treating symptoms. If the AI generates code you don't understand, ask the AI to explain it (it can often do this surprisingly well!) – or, if in doubt, rewrite it yourself so you have full control.

- **Targeted and Conscious Use:** Use AI strategically where it has strengths and the risk is low: for generating boilerplate code, rapidly prototyping UI elements, creating standard patterns (e.g., data access layers), assisting with debugging through error finding or explanation, or learning new concepts. Be significantly more cautious and critical with complex, domain-specific business logic, security-critical code sections, or decisions affecting the core architecture of the system. Not everything the AI *can* do, it *should* be allowed to do.

- **Testing as an Indispensable Safety Net:** Comprehensive, automated tests are the best means to objectively ensure that the (also AI-generated) code does what it's supposed to do and doesn't introduce unwanted side effects or regressions. Test-Driven Development (TDD) or Behavior-Driven Development (BDD) can be particularly valuable approaches here: they force clear definition of requirements and expected behavior *before* the AI generates code. The tests then serve as an executable specification and an automatic check for the AI's output.

The principle: Autopilot is great, but replacing the pilot? Not a good idea, at least not for passenger planes and critical software. The final decision, the strategic direction, and the ultimate responsibility must remain with the human – the AI is just the (sometimes brilliant, sometimes naive) co-pilot who can assist us.

Practical Application: Where AI Shines and Where It Stumbles (with Example)

Let's talk specifics: When does it make sense to jump on the "vibe" train, and when is it better to stick to the good old manual way? The art lies in realistically assessing the strengths and weaknesses of the current AI generation.

Where AI (currently) makes sense and can really help:

- **Prototyping & MVPs:** As mentioned multiple times, often unbeatable for quickly visualizing and testing ideas without weeks of groundwork.

- **Boilerplate & Standard Code:** Generating CRUD operations, setting up projects from templates, creating standard UI components (buttons, forms, tables), writing simple unit tests (e.g., for getters/setters or basic logic), implementing well-known, well-documented algorithms (e.g., standard sorting methods).

- **Code Translation & Modernization:** "Translate this old Java code to Python" or "Modernize this

JavaScript code to ES6 syntax." Can be a very good starting point for tackling legacy code, but requires intensive manual review and rework.

- **Learning & Documentation:** Having code explained ("What does this cryptic function do?"), generating examples for design patterns or using unfamiliar libraries, drafting docstrings or comments as a starting point.
- **Simple Scripts & Automations:** Small helpers for data conversion, file processing, simple API queries, or automating repetitive tasks.
- **Refactoring Support:** Getting suggestions for code simplification, consistent renaming of variables or methods, extracting code blocks into functions (but always critically review if the extraction makes sense!).

Where AI (currently) often doesn't help, hits limits, or even harms:

- **Complex, Novel Algorithms:** When it comes to truly innovative solutions for which there are few or no examples in the training data, AI will struggle to go beyond known patterns. True algorithmic creativity is rare.

- **Deep, Nuanced Domain Logic:** Business rules that are very specific to a company or industry, full of exceptions, historically grown complexity, and implicit knowledge often require deep human understanding that AI (currently) lacks. The risk of misinterpretation by the AI is high here.

- **High-Performance or Safety-Critical Code:** When every millisecond counts (e.g., high-frequency trading, game engines) or an error could have catastrophic consequences (e.g., in medical software, flight control, critical infrastructure), blindly trusting AI code is absolutely unacceptable. Human expertise, rigorous testing, and often formal verification methods are essential here.

- **Debugging Subtle or System-Wide Errors:** Race conditions, deadlocks, memory leaks, unexpected interactions between distributed system components – such errors often require deep system understanding, creative troubleshooting, and the ability to think across module boundaries, which usually goes beyond the capabilities of current AIs.

- **Large-Scale Architectural Decisions:** Strategic planning of the overall architecture of a complex system, weighing long-term trade-offs between different approaches (e.g., microservices vs. monolith), considering maintainability, scalability, and future flexibility – this remains a central human domain requiring experience and foresight.

- **Tasks Requiring Empathy or Deep Contextual Understanding:** Truly good UI/UX design that empathizes with the user and anticipates their needs, or understanding implicit requirements and nuances from conversations with stakeholders – human, social, and emotional intelligence are (still) clearly superior here.

Speed & Example: The "Instant" App?

So, can you really build an app without writing a line of code? Theoretically, for very simple cases, maybe. Let's imagine we want to build a simple To-Do app with Vue.js, host it on Firebase, with deployment via GitHub Actions. The "Vibe Coding" approach might look like this:

1. **Prompt App Structure:** "Create a simple Vue.js 3 To-Do app using the Composition API. It should have a component to display the list (TodoList.vue), a component to add new todos (AddTodoForm.vue), and a component for individual todo items (TodoItem.vue). Use Pinia for state management (store for todos with actions to load, add, delete, toggle completion status). Todos should be markable as done and deletable." -> AI generates the basic structure, components, store.

2. **Prompt Firebase Integration:** "Add Firebase (Firestore) to store the todos. Write service functions in firebaseService.js to load all todos, add a new todo, update the completion status, and delete a todo in a Firestore collection named 'todos'. Initialize Firebase using environment variables (VITE_FIREBASE_CONFIG) for configuration." -> AI generates Firebase setup and service code.

3. **Prompt Deployment:** "Create a GitHub Actions workflow file (.github/workflows/deploy.yml) triggered on push to the main branch. It should

set up Node.js, install dependencies (npm install), build the Vue app (npm run build), and deploy the dist directory to Firebase Hosting using the FirebaseExtended/action-hosting-deploy@v0 action. The FIREBASE_TOKEN and FIREBASE_PROJECT_ID should be provided as GitHub Secrets." -> AI generates the YAML file. Sounds magical, right? Almost too good to be true. And here comes the inevitable catch: **You still need to know damn well what you're doing!**

- You need to understand what Vue.js, the Composition API, Pinia, Firebase, Firestore (including security rules!), GitHub Actions, and the principle of CI/CD are. You need to know the concepts.
- You need to critically review the generated code parts: Is the component structure sensible? Is the state management approach correct and efficient? Is the Firebase code secure (keyword: Firestore Rules!) and performant? Is important error handling or input validation missing? Does the code meet project standards?

- You need to do all the configuration: Create a Firebase project, enable Hosting, create a Firestore database and (very importantly!) define secure rules, create a GitHub repository, correctly set up the necessary secrets (FIREBASE_TOKEN, FIREBASE_PROJECT_ID) in GitHub, tell the AI the correct variable names and configuration details.
- You need to thoroughly test the result: Does the app work as expected in all scenarios? Does the deployment work reliably? Are there security vulnerabilities?
- You need to debug when something goes wrong – and it most likely will at some point. The AI might help, but troubleshooting and finding the solution require your understanding.

The AI might save you from typing many lines, but not from thinking, planning, configuring, critically reviewing, testing, and debugging. You act as the architect, the technical lead, the quality manager – you direct the AI. The enormous speed comes from radically accelerating the *implementation* of known patterns and standard tasks. The *total time* to create a *production-ready, high-quality* product, however, is still largely determined by human expertise in planning, design, architecture, testing, integration, and project management. A simple app might indeed be created in a day instead of a week this way, but a complex, business-critical application still requires careful human work and expertise.

Conclusion on Practice: Great for standard stuff and prototypes, flop for complex or critical systems (at least without massive oversight and expertise).

Knowing when to "vibe" and when to roll up your sleeves and dive deep yourself is the real art of modern software engineering.

Table: Vibe Coding – Overview of Advantages vs. Risks

Advantages	Risks
Higher Development Speed	Lack of Code Quality & Inconsistency
Rapid Prototyping & MVP Creation	Difficult Maintainability & High Technical Debt
Increased Developer Productivity	Security Vulnerabilities from Insecure Patterns/Defaults
Automation of Routine Tasks	Debugging Nightmare due to Lack of Understanding
Lower Barrier to Entry (Democratization)	Erosion of Fundamental Programming Skills
Support for Learning & Understanding	Dependency on AI Tools
Fostering Creativity & Experimentation	Scalability Problems due to Lack of Architecture
Potentially Smaller Teams Needed	Loss of Junior Positions / Chicken-and-Egg Problem
Focus on Higher-Level Tasks	Ethical Concerns (Bias, Privacy, Copyright)

Rethinking Education: Teaching Competencies for the AI Age

As discussed in Chapter 6, Vibe Coding presents major challenges for education. It's no longer enough just to teach programming. Curricula need to adapt:

- **Strengthen Fundamentals:** Paradoxically, fundamental concepts (algorithms, data structures, architecture, operating systems, networks) become even more important for evaluating and understanding AI output. These basics must be taught solidly.

- **Build AI Competence:** Students need to learn how LLMs work (at least basically), how to prompt effectively, how to use AI tools responsibly, and where their limits lie. AI literacy becomes a basic competency.

- **Focus on Higher-Order Skills:** Critical thinking, problem-solving, systems thinking, design and architecture, communication, and collaboration (including with AI) must take center stage more strongly.

- **Practice with Judgment:** Using AI tools in exercises and projects can be useful, but not as a substitute for independent thinking and implementation. Educators need to design tasks that promote understanding, not just skillful copying of AI-generated code. Perhaps through more complex problem statements, more focus on design and justification of decisions, or tasks where the AI deliberately hits its limits.

- **Promote Lifelong Learning:** The most important skill will be the ability to continuously adapt to new tools and paradigms. Education should awaken and foster curiosity and the ability to learn independently.

The direction for education: Rote learning was yesterday. The future needs developers who learn how to learn, think critically, and master AI as a tool, rather than being mastered by it.

Ethics and Guidelines: Rules of the Game for the New Era

With great power comes great responsibility. The use of AI in software development also raises ethical questions that we cannot ignore:

- **Bias in Data and Algorithms:** AI models learn from data that can contain human biases. How do we ensure that AI-generated code is not discriminatory or reinforces existing inequalities?

- **Transparency and Explainability:** Can we understand why the AI suggests a particular piece of code? Who is responsible if AI-generated code causes errors or harm? The question of accountability is central.

- **Data Privacy:** How do we securely handle data used in prompts or processed by AI tools? Where is this data stored, and who has access to it? (See also security tips in Chapter 5).

- **Intellectual Property:** Who owns the code generated by the AI? Is it based on copyrighted code from the training data? The legal frameworks here are often still unclear.

- **Impact on the Job Market:** What responsibility do we as an industry have towards developers whose jobs might be endangered by AI? How do we manage the transition fairly?

The ethical compass: With great power comes... exactly. Bias, privacy, responsibility – we need to build the ethical guardrails for AI in code now, before development overtakes us and creates facts on the ground.

Chapter 8: The Great Tremor – Socioeconomic Consequences of Vibe Coding

So far, we've focused heavily on the technical aspects and the direct impact on us developers. But the AI wave in software development is more than just a new toolset – it has the potential to trigger profound socioeconomic shifts. So let's zoom out and look at the bigger picture: How could Vibe Coding change the economy and society?

The Job Market in a Blender: Who Wins, Who Loses?

Arguably the most hotly debated question: Is AI taking our jobs? The answer, as usual, is complicated.

- **Shift, Not (Just) Destruction:** As touched upon in Chapter 6, certain roles and tasks will likely come under pressure. Routine coding, simple

89

test cases, perhaps even parts of junior-level support could become more automated. At the same time, new roles are emerging: Prompt Engineers, AI Validators, specialists in AI security and ethics, people who train and maintain AI models. So, it's more likely a massive *shift* in skills and job profiles.

- **Salary Polarization?** It's conceivable that demand (and thus compensation) for top architects, AI experts, and developers with deep domain knowledge will increase, as they need to design complex systems and direct the AI. Simultaneously, developers with more generalist or easily automatable skills could face greater wage pressure. The gap could widen.
- **Freelancers & Gig Economy:** For freelancers, AI could be a blessing (higher productivity, more projects possible) but also intensify competition and drive down prices for standard tasks. The ability to use AI effectively and offer higher-value services (consulting, architecture) will be crucial.
- **The "Human Touch":** Tasks requiring creativity, empathy, complex problem-solving, and a deep

understanding of human needs (e.g., UX design, complex requirements analysis, strategic product decisions) will likely remain human domains for the foreseeable future.

The forecast: The job market will definitely change. There will be winners and losers. Adaptability, lifelong learning, and focusing on higher-value, less easily automated skills will be vital for survival.

Economic Turbulence: Productivity Boom or Power Concentration?

The impact on the overall economy could also be significant, and opinions vary widely.

- **The Hoped-For Productivity Boost:** This is the great promise. If software – the lubricant of the modern economy – can indeed be developed significantly faster, cheaper, and perhaps even better, it could trigger an enormous productivity surge. Companies could innovate faster, offer new digital services, and make internal processes more efficient. From a macroeconomic perspective, this *could* lead to higher growth and prosperity. Especially for old economies like Germany, often seen as lagging in digitalization, this presents a huge opportunity. Could AI-assisted development help alleviate the shortage of skilled workers, accelerate the modernization of public administration, or enable the much-discussed Mittelstand (SMEs) to leap into the digital age? The hope is there, but implementation is complex, and actual productivity gains are often hard to measure and depend on many factors (code quality, integration effort, etc.). Flanking measures in education and infrastructure are needed to realize this potential.

- **Startup Boom or Just More of the Same?** The theory goes: Lower development costs and faster prototyping cycles lower barriers to entry. This could theoretically lead to a wave of new startups disrupting established markets with innovative ideas. More competition, more dynamism. The flip side: Does this really create *better* products or just *faster-built* ones? Do these startups easily find funding, or do VCs prefer to bet on established players with proven (albeit slower) methods? And how many of these quickly "vibed" MVPs survive the first market test or fail due to scaling and maintenance issues? It's conceivable that we'll see more startups, but the success rate won't necessarily increase if the quality or business model isn't sound.

- **The Danger of Power Concentration:** This is perhaps the biggest economic concern. Developing and training the most powerful AI models (especially large LLMs) requires immense resources – computing power, data, and capital. These resources are concentrated in the hands of a few global tech giants (Alphabet/Google, Microsoft/OpenAI, Meta, Amazon, etc.). If these companies control the underlying models and the best development platforms, they could gain enormous market power. Smaller software houses, startups, and individual developers might become heavily dependent on these platforms (vendor lock-in). While they benefit from the tools, they might pay high prices (directly or indirectly through data) or have to submit to the rules and API changes of the platform operators. Furthermore, the data generated by using the tools flows back to the major providers, further improving their models – a self-reinforcing cycle (network effect) that makes it extremely difficult for new competitors. Open-source AI models (like Llama, Mistral, etc.) could provide an important counterweight here, promoting more competition and transparency, but their development and maintenance also require significant effort and community support to keep up technologically and economically.

- **Emergence of New Business Models:** Beyond optimizing existing processes, AI development could also enable entirely new markets and business models. Hyper-personalized software solutions tailored to each individual user – something previously often too costly – become conceivable. Or specialized AI agents offering complex but repetitive development tasks (e.g., certain types of code audits, performance optimizations) as a service. Perhaps new services will emerge around the training, validation, and ethical assessment of AI systems that generate code. Micro-SaaS (Software as a Service for niche problems) could experience another boost as development costs decrease.

- **The Software Pricing Puzzle:** What happens to the cost of software? Logically: If development becomes more efficient, prices should fall. But reality is more complex. Providers could use productivity gains to increase their margins, especially if they have a strong market position. Or they might adopt value-based pricing – the price is based on the perceived value to the customer (e.g., time saved, new features enabled), not the production cost. A further shift towards subscription models, where access to the latest AI features (e.g., in the code editor) costs extra and increases dependency on the provider, is also conceivable. It's unlikely that software will become universally cheaper; rather, pricing models and value propositions will likely shift.

The economic paradox: Vibe Coding promises efficiency and innovation, **offers the chance to drive national digitalization,** but also carries the risk of increased monopolization and unequal distribution of gains. Finding the balance will be a major challenge for business and politics.

Society in Transition: Between Digital Divide and New Opportunities

The changes aren't limited to the job market and the economy; they seep deeper into society, raising fundamental questions:

- **The Digital Divide 2.0 – The Skill Gap:** There's a legitimate concern that the divide will no longer just be between those who have internet access and those who don't, but between those who can *competently use* AI tools and those who cannot. It's not just about entering a prompt, but about critically evaluating the results, strategically deploying the tools, and understanding the pitfalls. Those who don't acquire these meta-skills – whether through formal education, further training, or self-initiative – could fall behind professionally and socially. This could exacerbate existing social inequalities, as access to high-quality (continuing) education is often unevenly distributed. The question is: How do we ensure broad access to these new competencies and prevent a "two-tier society" of AI users and non-users?

- **Democratization vs. Control – Who Holds the Reins?** On one hand, there's the promise of democratization: More people can create software, citizen initiatives can build their own tools, small businesses can develop digital solutions that were previously unaffordable. This sounds like empowerment and diversity, like a "maker" culture on steroids. On the other hand, there's the reality of the platform economy: The most powerful AI models and development environments are controlled by a few large corporations. When we use their tools, we simultaneously feed their systems with data and become dependent on their APIs, pricing models, and terms of service. Is there a danger that this central control could lead to less transparency, potential censorship (what kind of code is allowed to be generated?), or the manipulation of information and code? The balance between using powerful central tools and fostering open, transparent, and perhaps decentralized alternatives (keyword: Open Source AI) will be crucial for future creative freedom.

- **Education System Under Pressure – More Than Just Learning to Prompt:** As discussed in Chapter 6, educational institutions face a mammoth task. It's not enough to introduce "Prompt Engineering" as a new subject or simply integrate AI tools into teaching. The entire approach needs to change: Away from rote memorization of syntax and facts, towards fostering critical thinking, problem-solving skills, creativity, ethical awareness, and the ability to collaborate – including with AI. This requires not only new curricula but also new teaching methods (project-based, interdisciplinary) and, above all, educators who are themselves proficient in using these technologies and understanding their implications. The necessity of lifelong learning becomes a basic requirement for almost all professions, which in turn raises questions about the funding, organization, and accessibility of continuing education opportunities for the entire population.

- **Potential for Misuse – The Dark Side of Code Generation:** Every powerful tool can be misused. AI that generates code is no exception. The easier creation of malware (viruses, ransomware), sophisticated phishing attacks, or tools for automated disinformation (e.g., bots spreading fake code or misleading technical analyses) is potentially facilitated. The generation of code for autonomous weapon systems or surveillance technologies also raises serious ethical questions, as development barriers could be lowered. An arms race is emerging between those using AI for malicious purposes and those trying to use AI to defend against these threats (e.g., AI-based security scanners that can also detect AI-generated malware). Regulating and controlling these risks is a complex global challenge involving technical, legal, and ethical dimensions.

The societal challenge: How do we ensure that the benefits of AI-assisted software development reach as many people as possible, while minimizing the risks (inequality, loss of control, misuse)? This requires a broad societal debate and smart policy frameworks that encourage innovation while establishing safeguards and ensuring access to education and participation.

Global Impacts: Is the Playing Field Shifting?

The AI revolution doesn't stop at national borders:

- **Offshoring & Outsourcing:** Traditional software offshoring models could change. As routine tasks become more automated, the focus might shift from pure cost savings to locations with highly skilled AI experts and architects who can design complex systems and manage AI tools. Conversely, AI tools could also make it easier to coordinate globally distributed teams and overcome language barriers, enabling new forms of international collaboration.

- **International Competition:** Countries and regions that quickly build strong AI competence (in research, application, and education) could gain significant competitive advantages. The "War for AI Talent" is already underway. **For Germany, the consistent use of AI in software development could be an opportunity to make up ground in the global digitalization race and strengthen technological sovereignty,** provided the framework conditions (education, infrastructure, investment) are right.
- **Access for Developing Countries:** Does the democratization through Vibe Coding offer developing countries new opportunities to make digital leaps and develop their own software solutions for local problems? Or will they become

more dependent users of technology from industrialized nations, further cementing existing global inequalities? Access to computing power, data, and know-how will be crucial here.

The global game: AI-powered software development will rearrange the global power dynamics in the tech industry and beyond. Those who master and wisely deploy the technology will have the edge.

In summary: The socioeconomic consequences of Vibe Coding are complex, multifaceted, and often contradictory. There are enormous opportunities, but also significant risks for jobs, economic structures, and social cohesion. A naive "technology solves everything" attitude is just as misplaced as outright rejection. We must closely monitor developments, ask the right questions, and actively shape the future.

Chapter 9: The Future Unfolds – Wave Riding for Software Professionals

We've reached the end of our journey through the world of Vibe Coding – or perhaps we're just at the beginning of a much larger wave. We've seen how this new way of programming is emerging, the tempting possibilities it offers, but also the deep pitfalls that can open up. As an experienced software professional, you've seen quite a few hypes come and go. You know that things are rarely as revolutionary as they're initially made out to be. But this time, you feel, it really could be different. Time for a conclusion and a look ahead.

Vibe Coding: A Rollercoaster Summary

What are the key takeaways?

- **It's real:** Vibe Coding is more than a buzzword. It's the manifestation of advances in LLMs applied to software development. The tools are here and improving rapidly.

- **It's powerful:** The potential for acceleration, democratization, and productivity gains is enormous. Especially in prototyping and for routine tasks, AI can be a real game changer.

- **It's risky:** Code without understanding, quality defects, maintenance nightmares, security holes, and the erosion of core competencies are real dangers we must take seriously. Blind faith in AI is naive and dangerous.

- **It changes our role:** The skills we need are shifting. Less pure typing, more prompting, evaluating, architecting, communicating, and critical thinking. The fundamentals remain important, but their application changes.

- **It requires responsibility:** We need clear processes, human oversight, adapted educational concepts, and ethical guardrails to use the technology meaningfully and safely.

- **It has far-reaching consequences:** The effects are not limited to technology but affect the job market, the economy, and society as a whole.

The rollercoaster ride between hype and horror, between fascination and fear, will likely accompany us for some time.

Gazing into the Crystal Ball: What's Next?

Predictions are always difficult, especially about the future (loosely based on Mark Twain or whoever). But a few trends seem to be emerging:

- **Even Smarter AI Agents:** AI will get even better at understanding context, working across entire projects, solving more complex tasks autonomously, and perhaps even proactively suggesting improvements to code and architecture.

- **Multimodal Development:** Interaction will go beyond text. We might communicate with AI using diagrams, sketches, voice, or even gestures.

- **Specialized AI Models:** Alongside general-purpose LLMs, specialized models for specific domains, languages, or tasks will likely emerge, delivering even more precise results.

- **Democratization Advances:** Even more people without a formal programming background will be able to create simple applications or automations. This could lead to an explosion of niche software.

- **The "Human-in-the-Loop" Remains Central:** Despite all advances, human expertise will remain indispensable for complex, creative, and critical tasks for the foreseeable future. AI will be more of a co-pilot than the sole pilot.
- **Focus on Verification and Validation:** With the increase in AI-generated code, tools and methods for checking, testing, and formally verifying this code will become increasingly important.
- **New Job Profiles Emerge:** Roles like "AI Prompt Engineer," "AI Quality Assurance Specialist," or "AI Ethics Officer" could become more important, while traditional developer roles continue to evolve.

Software development will continue to change, probably faster than ever before. And that leads us to an important digression...

Digression: The Holy Grail and Pandora's Box – AGI and ASI

So far, we've primarily discussed the current generation of AI – the so-called "Narrow AI" systems or specialized AIs. LLMs that generate code, image recognition systems, translation tools – they are all extremely good at *one* specific task, but not universally intelligent. Vibe Coding is a product of this Narrow AI. But on the horizon (or perhaps just in the minds of some researchers and science fiction authors) loom two larger concepts:

- **AGI (Artificial General Intelligence):** This is the often-cited "holy grail" of AI research. An AGI would be an AI with human-like cognitive abilities, capable of learning and performing *any* intellectual task a human can. It could think across contexts, be creative, solve problems in entirely new ways. When (or if) AGI will be achieved is the subject of fierce debate. Some believe it's only a few years away, others think decades or even centuries, and still others consider it fundamentally impossible.

- **ASI (Artificial Superintelligence):** This is the next level – and potentially Pandora's Box. An ASI would be an intelligence that *far* surpasses human intelligence in practically all relevant domains. Its capabilities would be almost unimaginable to us. The potential consequences of ASI are extreme: It could solve humanity's biggest problems (cure diseases, stop climate change, end poverty) or pose an existential threat if its goals are not perfectly aligned with ours (the famous "alignment problem").

What does this have to do with Vibe Coding?

At first glance, not much. Vibe Coding uses today's specialized LLMs. But the rapid development of these LLMs is a driver of the AGI debate. Some see the ever-improving language and coding abilities as the first sparks of more general intelligence.

Should AI actually develop towards AGI or even ASI, the impact on software development (and everything else) would be fundamental and barely predictable. Perhaps an AGI would "understand" and "write" software in a way that makes our current methods completely obsolete. Maybe human developers wouldn't be needed at all, just someone to give the AGI high-level goals. Perhaps an ASI could even generate code that improves and evolves itself.

This is all highly speculative. But it's important to keep these long-term perspectives in mind when discussing the current AI wave. Vibe Coding might just be the first harbinger of a much larger transformation. It shows us how quickly things can change and how crucial it is to accompany development critically and proactively.

The great unknown: Vibe Coding, driven by today's "Narrow AI," might just be the prelude. The real revolution could only come with AGI or ASI – with consequences we can hardly imagine today.

Final Thoughts: Between Fascination and Responsibility

As a software professional, you are right in the middle of this storm. It's exciting, no question. The possibility of implementing ideas faster, freeing oneself from tedious routine work, and perhaps even creating entirely new kinds of software is fascinating. It tickles the playful instinct and the spirit of innovation.

At the same time, however, you also feel the responsibility. The responsibility for the quality, security, and maintainability of the systems you design or contribute to. The responsibility towards the users who rely on these systems. And perhaps also the responsibility towards the profession and the next generation of developers.

Vibe Coding is like a powerful new technology – a jackhammer where we might have only had a hammer before. You can build faster and more efficiently with it, but you can also break a lot more if you don't know what you're doing.

The key is to stay curious but not naive. To try out the

new tools, leverage their strengths, but always keep their weaknesses and risks in mind. Not to forget the fundamentals, but to use them as a compass in this new landscape. And above all: to continue using your own judgment, thinking critically, and taking ultimate responsibility for the outcome.

The wave is coming, that much is certain. Whether we get swept away by it or learn to ride it is up to us. It's a challenge, yes. But for someone accustomed to designing complex systems and constantly adapting to new technologies, it might also be exactly the kind of challenge that makes the job exciting. Let's tackle it – with reason and perhaps also a bit of vibe.

About the Author

Growing up near Hamburg, Germany, the fascination with technology was a constant companion from an early age. After studying Business Informatics in the tranquil town of Wedel, the  path led directly to where bits and bytes feel at home: software development.

As part of various software architect teams, the author not only dove deep into the diverse aspects of software creation but also developed a passion for constantly questioning things and improving them. Always searching for new ways, better processes, and technologies that make life (or at least coding) easier. It's no wonder, then, that the topic of Artificial Intelligence, especially its entry into software development, sparked intense interest. The possibilities seem limitless, the speed breathtaking. Yet, as with any powerful technology, fascination is mixed with a healthy dose of concern and skepticism. It is precisely this blend of curiosity, experience, and the feeling that something big is happening here (for better or worse) that prompted this book – an attempt to illuminate the emerging wave of "Vibe Coding" from the pragmatic perspective of a software professional who has seen a tech wave or two come and go.

Thank You!